REBOUND

IF YOU CAN

BY S. E. MCKENZIE

DEDICATION
To everyone who has been left out in the cold

THIS BOOK IS A BOOK OF SPECULATIVE FICTION
Characters, companies, governments, places, events, are either products of the author's imagination or used fictitiously. Any resemblance to persons (living or dead), companies, governments, places and/or events, is a coincidence and unintended.

TABLE OF CONTENTS

ReBound

I

The sunrise stayed for the day;
Then set in the usual way;
The door was open

Like it never had been before;

Water was dripping and it was all over the floor;
I did not know from where
And I couldn't find anyone who would care.

The fog crept in
And I lost my way
No one listened to a word I had to say.

So alone;
My heart felt like stone;
The tide was coming in

And no one would let me win;
That was the day after
The Starman died;

The day a noble and a gentle man was pulled
Back into his new home
In the sky.

For it was his turn to fly
To a place
One could never reach alive.

All he left me was the starlight
That I could only see
During the night

When I could not sleep
And could not dream
When the silence made me want to scream.

II
Such a brave Contradiction
Against the Pull
Which drives us

To flow against the tides;
Inside out
No one left to shout out for me

ReBound

For the Starman
Could now
Defy gravity

In dignity;

The same Force
Which kept me
Grounded on this Earth.

But left me all alone
Now it was up to me
To grow wings of my own.

And the Lady with the Rose
Saw the light too
That the Starman had left behind

To shine light onto my paths
And to warm my heart
So I would not drown

In the ocean deep inside
Pulling me
From tide to tide.

The light that Starman left behind
Strengthened
My heart

Still pulsating
When torn apart;
That was the power

Of his light upon my heart.

III

The Starman would now discover
Our Universal Source.
There might be one;

There might be another;

Few would ever know;
A Source more than a Super Ego
Clashing into the night;

Picking a fight
With those who could never win
Without the Lady with the Rose;

We waited until she arose

ReBound

In the aftermath;
When manufacturing despair
Was meant to take over the loser's mind;

We found
A way
To rebound;

Now stuck
On this dead end street
In this dead end town;

Manufactured to be that way;

When we lost our right of way;
We could not progress; while those
On the other side of the tracks

Just turned away;
Never having anything good to say; to us;
They could not see the Lady with the Rose

Who arose
From the aftermath
That was left behind.

They could watch but could not see
The dead end road to Snobocracy;
Some were below and some were above

In this dead end town
There was too much hate
And not enough love.

So I looked up above
And saw the starlight
That the Starman had left behind;

With us;
For now he was living somewhere above
This tortured land

Under the command
Of money and gold
Tattered and torn

While allegiance was sworn
To the Carrot-stick God
That we could never see;

Some had sworn a life of secrecy;
For Money had written
In God We Trust

ReBound

All over it;
The bill was our life line
So we knew that we must

Have blind trust
If we were to rebound
From Zero.

IV

It was early in the morning;
So we were able to
Avoid the swarming.

I saw so much food
I could not believe my eyes;
Half of it had been discounted too;

I was going to buy some just for you.
Then I heard someone say
That the food must be thrown away

For food costs more than people can pay.
Devaluation; a hurt sensation;
Was the only way; in a land crippled in hate and debt;

Economy zombified;
Another Grumpy old Man
Had just lied;

Another starving child had just died;
"The worst was yet to come,"
I heard the Grumpy Old Man say

As he pushed a blue trolley carrying all the food away;
Then I saw many more Grumpy Old Men;
Here and there and everywhere;

Too bitter to have a gentle touch;
For their anger
Protected them from the fear

That was so near
And bombarded space
Here and there and everywhere.

They took all the food away and there was so much;
I asked why;
And the Grumpy Old Man said, 'That is the rule;

ReBound

To not obey makes you a fool; the food has expired
And will be thrown away."
The Grumpy Old Man's hate made him so tired

Soon he too would be expired.

V

In this land of snow
The Mechanized Warlords
Told the rest of us where to go;

Thrown over the fence;
Without a defence;
Nothing made sense.

As the Dead Cat
Bounced back; it rebounded from Zero;
Defying the negative trend;

Momentarily;
Thought it had found
A long lost friend

In a Sleeping Bear.
Just another loop
Leading to a dead end.

Just another wall
To confine youth;
As the dictator

Tried to break her mind;
The Lady with the Rose
Who had arose

Understood the value of self-worth;
While Nouveau Gestapo screamed into the night
The Starman was above sharing his light

During another act of war below;
Crushing self esteem
Destroying the dream;

Adaption to insane society
Made many turn away
For there was no inn

ReBound

Or home
To begin
The journey from.

While the Starman shone his light
Onto our path
The Lady with the Rose

Cried tears from above
When she saw the sorrow creep into tomorrow;
The aftermath of another act of war.

VI

Some said they could believe
In what they could not;
Some said hypocrisy

Was better than doubt;
Others said the truth
Would never be let out;

For what we had never seen,
We could not perceive;
Some lied anyway

To belong to the gang
Who jumped over the fence
Every Sunday night;

To start a fight
With those who could never win
But were left behind;

Bruised and accused;
Caught in the loop
That had no end.

As the Dead Cat
Bounced off the wall to rebound from Zero;
It thought it had found a friend

In the raging bull.

VII

If only the Starman could
Come down to join us
One more time

We would dance our youth away;
For we know our youth will not stay
And one day it will fade away;

ReBound

And make room for the new;
If only the Starman
Could tell us what he knew;

Then we would know
If there was anything at all
Behind the wall

Between life and death;
The circle which spins Infinity;
A space where we have no breath

Left to share;
Beyond
The grave,

If he could tell us
About the things beyond matter
We might feel more brave

And grow to be less sadder;

We would listen now; too;
So curious about what he knew
And where he had been;

While our hearts pound
He may hear our sound
Then we will know part of him

Is still around;
Near our ground;
For the life cycle seems to be

Always round.

If he could tell us
What he has seen;
We would then know

If Heaven was just a dream;

What we know
And what we sew
Will surely grow

From Today into Tomorrow;
While the tears falling from the sky
Reminded us that the Lady with the Rose

Would never impose.
Even though she could see all the acts of war;
More Brutal than ever before;

ReBound

Left many without a home
With a heart now as cold as stone;
And how could we care

For the Universal Force
Which kept our heart pounding
So mysteriously;

So mightily
Could Unify
Those trapped in the Domain ruled by the Lie.

Still the Universal Force could bind;
Make us more kind;
Less blind than the grumpy old master-mind.

If Starman didn't mind.

If I could only know
What Starman was doing now
I would see

What it was really like to be free,
To be
You and me.

VIII

I had to be true to me;
I could not lie
About what I could not see

Just to belong;
It was wrong
Did not make me strong

Though I would have let
Starman borrow
A tomorrow

From me
If it could have been done;
It would have been like

Having the power to share the sun;

Though the control freaks
Would never understand
Things they could not command

For life was above supply and demand.
Thought they were connected
To the power up above

ReBound

They forgot about love
So they did not care
How they shaped fate everywhere.

While the Lie would string us along;

And I could never feel
Or touch the space inside infinity;
So electrifying while still alive;

Possibly terrifying to those left behind on Earth;
Still trapped in hypocrisy;
They watched but could not see;

They said they knew
People they would never talk to;
Growing hypocrisy on the dead end street;

Slum power to dehumanize;
Gave the grumpy old man energy;
As he lived another day while dodging decay.

There was no other way;
He was rotting day by day;
Hidden in his Snobocracy;

The dead end mind knew no other way;
Now willfully blind;
Doing things that were more than just unkind.

The tyranny
Of negativity
Would shut out the power

To renew
Me and you
That Unknown Force for ever free

The power Starman tried to share
Once he knew
He was ready to climb into Infinity too;

Electrifying sometimes terrifying;
The Force we could only know;
After we pass; we would be free

From this world where few
Could really care
For they did not dare.

ReBound

IX

The air was polluted
And so was the heart
Behind the wall;

Looking down
So tall;
Making us

Feel so small.
As Starman
Was looking down

Smiling radiantly
We could not see
For the light

Would blind our eyes.
Pure light so bright;
For it was Starlight;

In the dead of night
It lit up everything in sight;
Until the sunrise brought in the new day

In the usual way;
The sun would stay
All day

And then the sun would set
And fade away.
Now we knew

What Starman was trying to say
While we all looked away;
For he was now home.

He had joined the source
Of all resource;
A new recourse.

For us too.

X

Politics of Dehumanization
Grab the ball; don't you fall;
The Sum Zero game must be played

To win;
If you lose
Pick up the pieces and go back

ReBound

To where it all began;
Though the cards are stacked
Against you;

In the fools game
Take the 1% chance
To leap ahead;

You must jump over the fence
To see what is over there
In the other world

Where Gestapo told us all
That we would fall
If we tried to belong;

But he was wrong;

For we are now one;
In one world
Still young;

Still growing
Into something new
From the energy Starman left behind.

Gave us strength so we would not drown
In the ocean inside
Pulling us from tide to tide.

For life
Was too short
To give up so soon;

For the sunshine
Would be here
By noon

And the God of War
Found
That the best feeling in the world

Was Love;
So he made a trade;
And all weapons were transformed

Into plowshares;
And there was Hunger
No more.

THE END

Produced by S.E. McKenzie Productions
First Print Edition February 2016

Enquiries: 1(778)992-2453
Mailing Address:
S. E. McKenzie Productions
168 B 5th St.
Courtenay, BC
V9N 1J4

Email Address:
messidartha@aol.com

http://www.amazon.com/SarahMcKenzie/e/B00H9RWX48/

www.ingramcontent.com/pod-product-compliance
Lightning Source LLC
Chambersburg PA
CBHW060548030426
42337CB00021B/4495